Through the Flowery Fence

Adventures in Florida

Through the Flowery Fence

Adventures in Florida

By

Irv Broughton

Illustrations by Lilly Ross

Open Look Books
Spokane, Washington

Through the Flowery Fence
Adventures in Florida

© 2022 by Irv Broughton

Open Look Books
Spokane, Washington

Book is available from Amazon, Kindle and fine Book Sellers.

For Information or to schedule speaking engagements:
www.irvbroughton.com

A whisper and then a silence:

Yet I know by their merry eyes

They are plotting and planning together

To take me by surprise.

From "The Children's Hour"
by Henry Wadsworth Longfellow

For Laken, Chase, Sadie and Lucille,
With Love

TOURING THE CHAIN OF LAKES

The lakes connect next to next

By hidden channels you didn't expect.

Shore bananas hung down by my neck.

As I picked one, I heard: "All hands on deck."

I wondered what snack could be next.

Peacocks

On Genius Drive, peacocks strut about

For visitors, with tails that opened out.

"It was always a grand show, as most tourists know.

I once found a loose feather. Now I, too, am aglow."

Dancing Palms

The dancing palms never took dance lessons,

But they dance like they've had two sessions.

"It's a dance marathon since the storm raged on,"

So claimed the wisdom from "Grandpa Don."

Within a day, the breezes called, "Stop!"

When the storm ended, the palms still swayed on,

As if happy and dancing to some secret song—

Or maybe it was love or the lovely blue dawn.

THE STUDY OF FIREFLIES

The study of fireflies is going to surprise.

"As the specks move closer," the scientist wrote,

"The lighted glow was something to note:

The night is a ship and the world's afloat."

THE BLACK PANTHER

A person from Dunedin sat there a-eatin'

Till a panther appeared just beyond.

He told the newspaper, "A kitty, it's not,

So I got out of the way and guess what?"

He tried to describe, but before long it was gone.

"But I'll tell you this: it was darker than dawn.

Black panthers are rare, so rarely we see,

I think I'll wait till it's in a movie."

THE NIGHT SPRINKLER

The sprinklers come on in the morn:
Who knew? Surely not the birds that adorn,
That rested, half-sleepy, there on the green,
Where one hunted worms it thought it had seen.

The spurt first surprised with slow flow,
Then the world exploded in a water show.
What are they doing? Why not up and go?

"I met the water you might know.
It rushed and sputtered as I ran through.
I suddenly felt like young birdies do.

Don't you sometimes shower to start the day?
Maybe birds like to copy and decided to stay."

HEMINGWAY'S HOUSE

Hemingway's house in Key West
Has cats everywhere taking rest.
They think it's a place of their own
Now that Hemingway's gone.

There were cats there once
When the writer lived there.
They're kittens of cats then
And a lot to compare.

They lounge on the porch.
They lounge on the lawn.

It's not green hills of Africa,
Let me make that quite clear.
But they stick around here
For year after year.

Some are quite spunky,
And some are quite tame.
I'm sure they're not writers,
But who can complain?
They have plenty to eat
And the Hemingway name.

The Sea View

I looked over at the ocean
And it stared back at me—
The wave, a half circle,
Telling me to flee.
I thought I might duck.
It was too late to run.

The coming wave blotted the sun.
The wave knew no bounds.
It was so plain to see.
A seashell went down:
With an *ockle, cockle, cockley.*

That heavyweight waited
And hung there in the air,
Giving me the time
To escape by a hair.

I'm not a good surfer
And waves come and go.
I'll wait for a small one,
Then go with the flow.

THE GRAND SEAFOOD MEAL

Dad ordered the Grand Seafood Meal:

Mussels and clams, crab legs and gumbo.

It came in a platter that truly was jumbo.

"Where do I start?" Dad proceeded to mumble.

He took one of each but it overflowed fork.

He tried to handle what looked like a stork.

A meal such as this needs a special handling.

He may need a hoist or a crane to be pulling.

When it all reached his mouth, he opened way wide.

"I feel like the seashore and here comes the tide!"

Through The Flowery Fence

I gave up something so I could see
Everyday beauty and mystery—
What I had not seen before:
Where's the entry, where's the door?

No offense when the fence grew full,
For I saw how at once how beautiful.
Because I wish beauty on everything,
I really love it when it's spring.

The essence of a thousand bees
We were, when seen down on our knees—
All the noses in the family—
A sniff away from the door knobby.

Searching where flowers in gate were worn,
We sniffed along for a smell less strong.
We had to find knobby before more flowers grow.
"Let us escape and go to the flower show."

FLORIDA COLD SNAP

The orange grove did escape snow,
But it froze so ice hung below.
Old Frosty blew cold breath all night,
And farmer woke in panic at the sight.

He saw two oranges frosty with beard,
Longer than ever before appeared.

It seems like Frosty had come to scold,
But some fruit held on, brave and bold.
The fruit is frozen and can't be sold.
"Quick! Drink it while it's icicle cold."

THE SPRING

The water flows millions of gallons per day
From a giant rock opening out of the way.
So much water: wonder what is at play?
I put in a boat but it floated away.

Thousands of gallons bubbling like soap
I heard a park ranger say, "Stay back of the rope."
To see it all better, I climbed the rock shelf.
There was one watery fairy and two dozen elves.

THE GATOR ESCALATOR

The gator escalator? Don't you dare.
For you, the gator does not care.

Quick, go away and go somewhere,
Where there you'll find a *real, real* stair.

It's the gator escalator,
But there's only one stop.

Be sure and get away
Before the big jaws drop.

FLUTTERING STRANGERS

Fluttering strangers are coming soon,
Their wings awakened by the sun and the moon.
Fluttering strangers, I'll know when I see.
They could be birds or most anybody.

Are they winter blossoms caught in breeze,
Ready to drop in the Gulf stream, by me,
Or perhaps "snowbirds" come South from the cold?
It's tourist time—it's January.

I can see yearly the friendly touristy:
Wintry, "snow-birdy," come-sunny company.

LYNNE RUTH'S BIRDCAGE

Lynne covered the birdcage with cloth,
So the parrot could sleep without light.
It woke and soon cawed, "Take it off—
It's now blocking my sight."

"Can we go to the window
To view places new?
It's glorious Florida!
More to see and to do."

THE SLEEPY AWNING

The sleepy awning that once held out the sun
Was worn and looked rather tattered and done,
But a person re-stitched it, hoped I'd hang on.
"If I just fixed the flap, it would surely last long."

But this stitch, this time, failed its design.
The wind came up and the flap collapsed.
Then the sun changed position: ZAPPITY-ZAP!
Down dropped the awning like a cat in my lap.

The Crayfish and The Playfish

The crayfish met a Playfish,
Who just wanted to play,
But the crayfish, by nature,
Kept on backing away.
"Why back away from us?"
Said Playfish, curious.
"The faster backward I go,
I'll feel like a skater in an ice show.
I'm not stand-off-fish,
For I'll walk if you wish.
Stroll, we will, the coral through
On spindly legs more than two."

"Is it not hard to keep track
Of what every leg wants to do?"

"No, I'd take pride in each stride alongside.
I'd love to be beside in the tide.
I'm only along for the ride."

THE BOOK CREATORS

Irv Broughton was born in the Sunshine State of Florida and grew up in Winter Park. He really loves the home state. As author of more than twenty books, he has written in a wide variety of genres, including poetry, song lyrics and screenplays–and in both fiction and non-fiction. Irv is author of two other children's books: *Walking Around Lucky: The Story of Sportswriter Red Smith* and *Gotcha! Watcha! Drugs are a Trap.* Another book, *The Lost Peninsula: Adventures in Florida as Told by the People Who Lived Them,* features interviews with forty-two old–time Floridians. A recent collection of poetry, *The Fires of Tangerine,* chronicles his early years.

Lilly Ross is an illustrator and art teacher. She resides in Seattle,Washington. A fan of the outdoors and adventure, her work focuses on nature and exploration. You can find her at www.waterlillyillustration.com

www.ingramcontent.com/pod-product-compliance
Lightning Source LLC
Chambersburg PA
CBHW042124030726
47599CB00002B/332